# Disney
# CINDERELLA

MUSIC FROM THE MOTION
PICTURE SOUNDTRACK

ISBN 978-1-4950-2215-9

Disney characters and artwork © Disney Enterprises, Inc.

## WALT DISNEY MUSIC COMPANY

DISTRIBUTED BY

## HAL•LEONARD®
CORPORATION

7777 W. BLUEMOUND RD. P.O. BOX 13819 MILWAUKEE, WI 53213

In Australia Contact:
**Hal Leonard Australia Pty. Ltd.**
4 Lentara Court
Cheltenham, Victoria, 3192 Australia
Email: ausadmin@halleonard.com.au

Visit Hal Leonard Online at
**www.halleonard.com**

# A GOLDEN CHILDHOOD

Music by PATRICK DOYLE

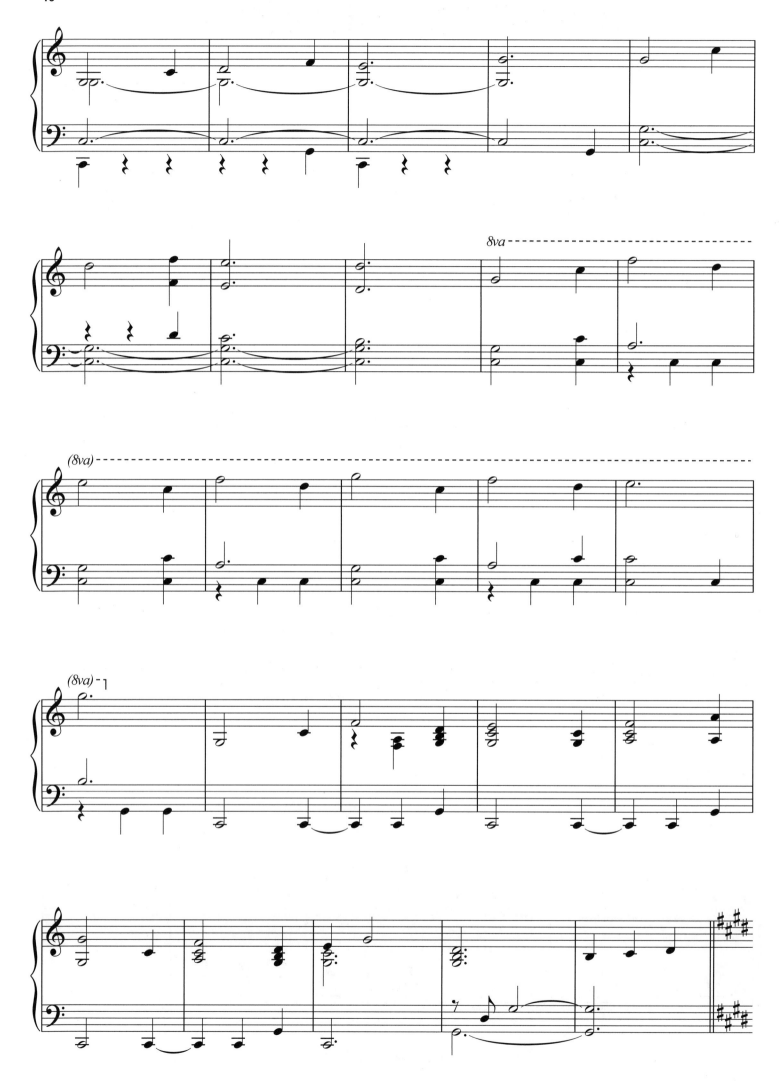

**Moderately**

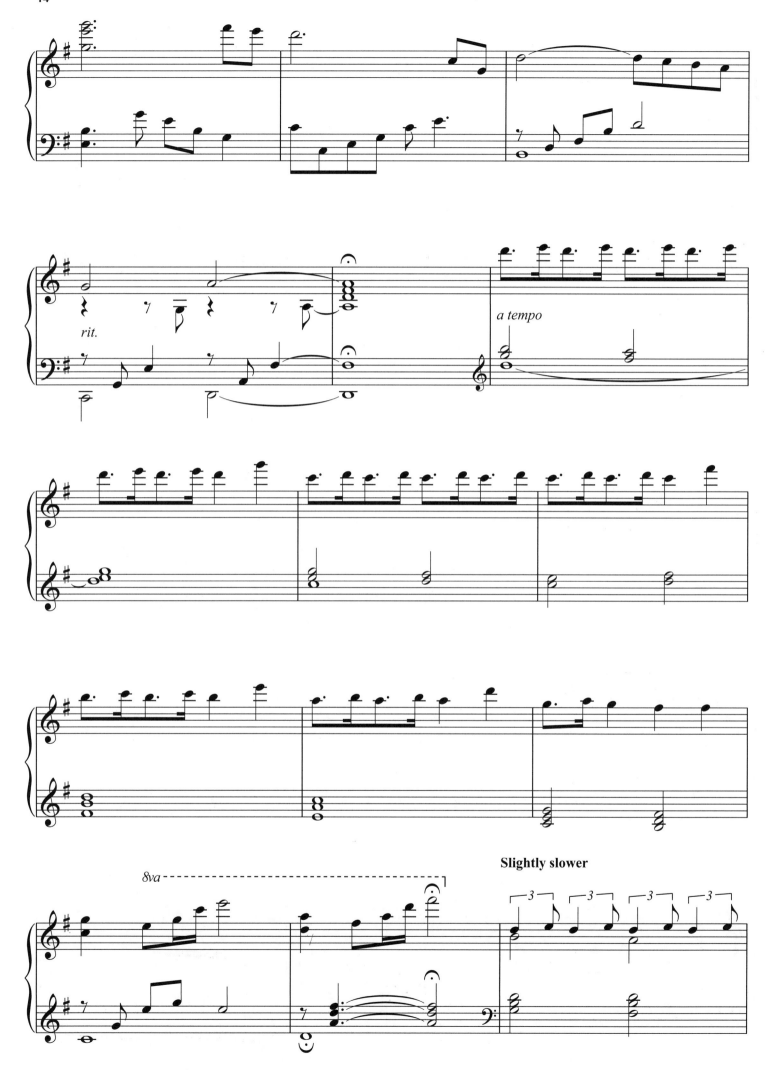

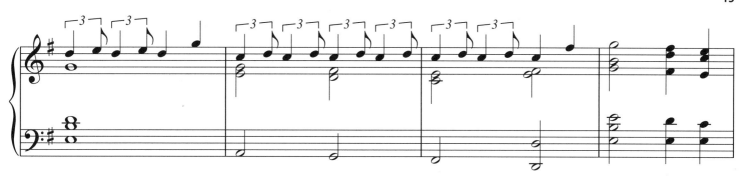

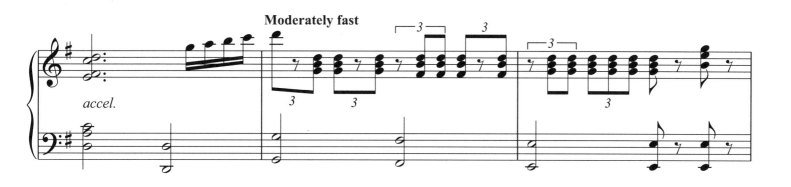

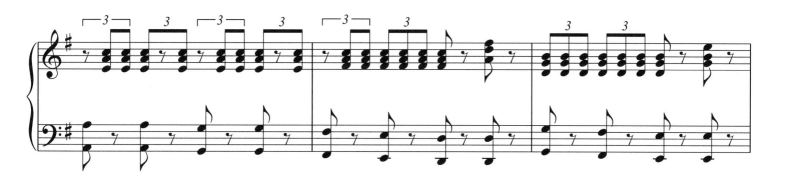

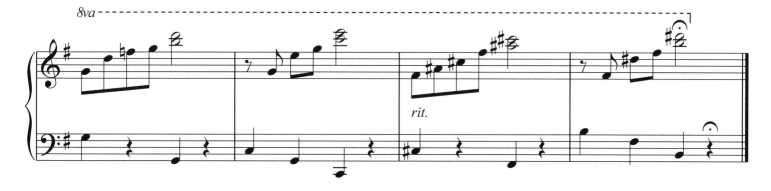

# THE FIRST BRANCH

Music by PATRICK DOYLE

**Moderately slow, expressively**

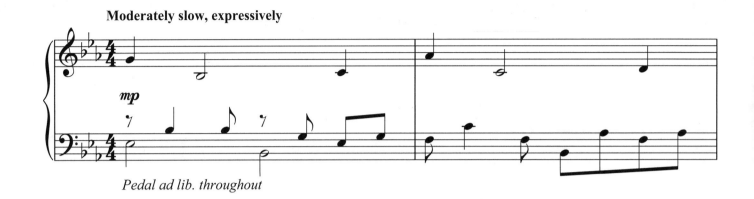

*Pedal ad lib. throughout*

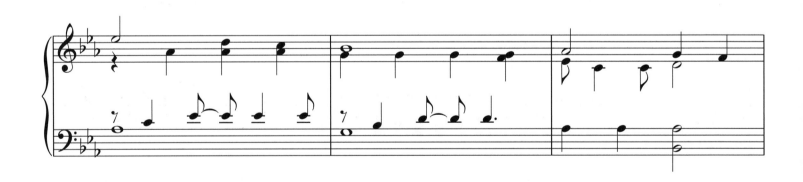

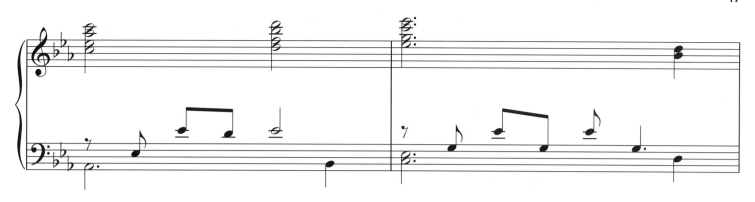

# LIFE AND LAUGHTER

Music by PATRICK DOYLE

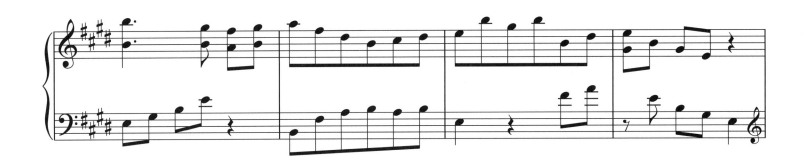

# RICH BEYOND REASON

Music by PATRICK DOYLE

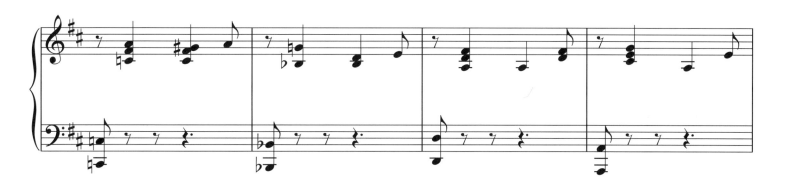

Moderately, in 2

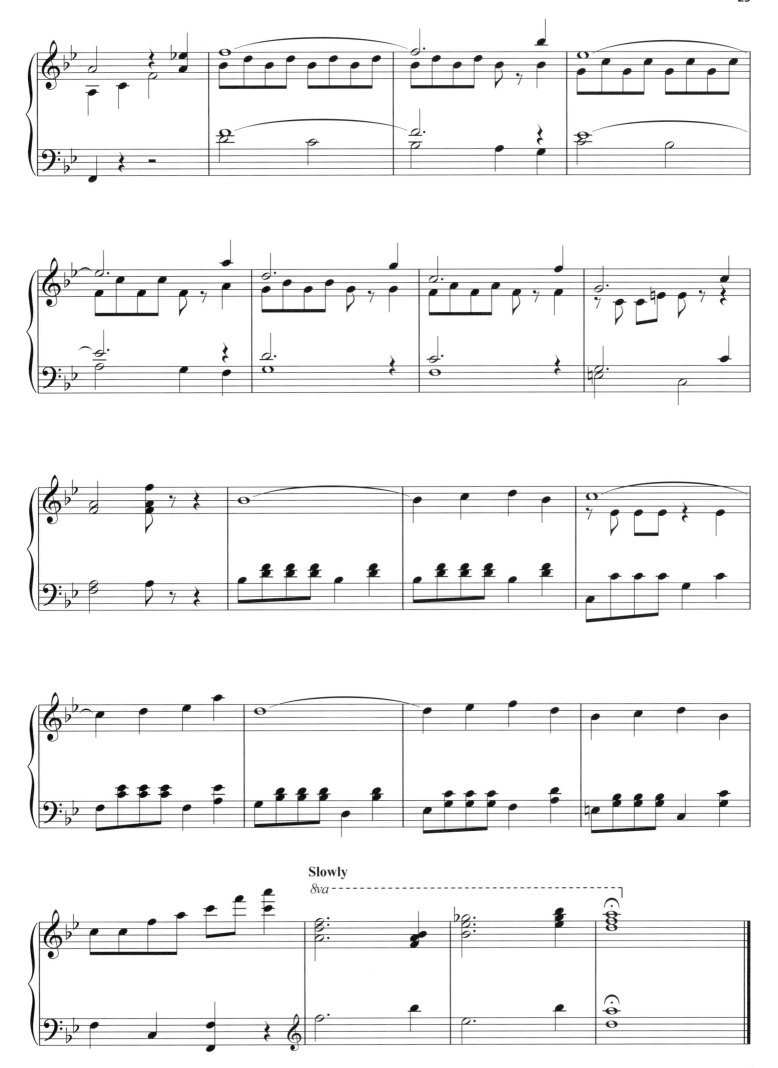

# VALSE ROYALE

Music by PATRICK DOYLE

**Moderately, in 1**

# WHO IS SHE

Music by PATRICK DOYLE

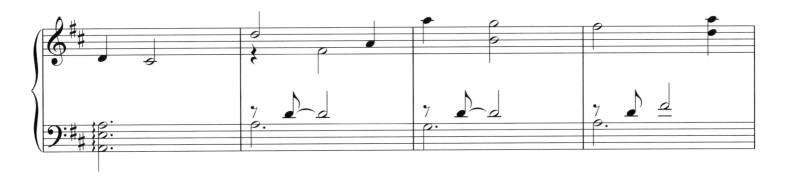

# LA VALSE CHAMPAGNE

Music by PATRICK DOYLE

To Coda ⊕

# LA POLKA DE PARIS

Music by PATRICK DOYLE

**Moderately fast, in 2**

# THE SLIPPER

Music by PATRICK DOYLE

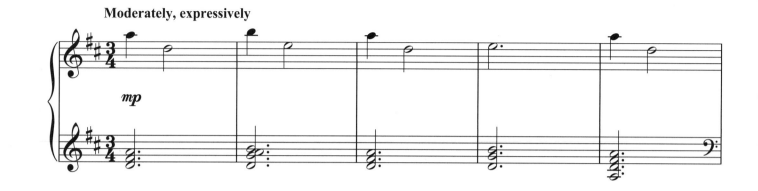

# SEARCHING THE KINGDOM

Music by PATRICK DOYLE

**Moderately fast**

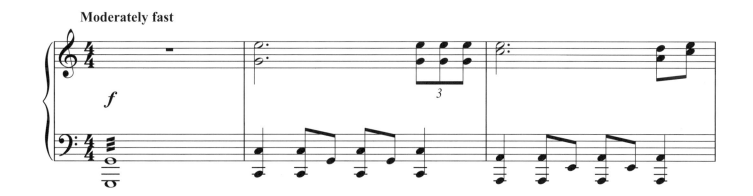

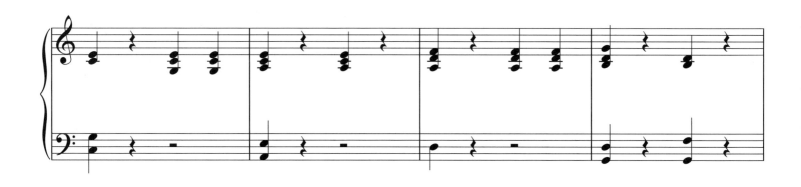

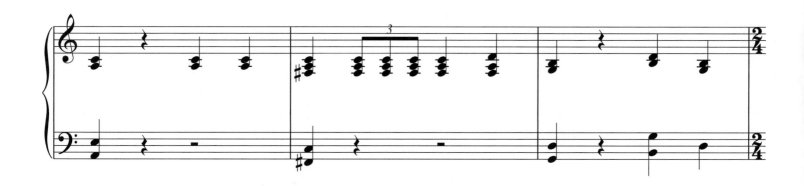

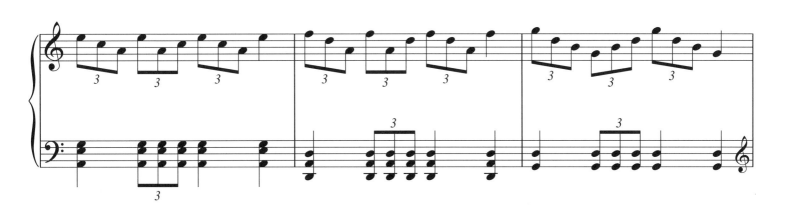

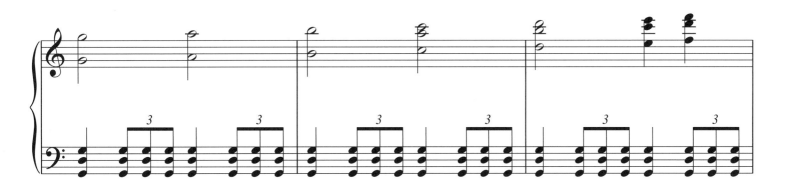

# A DREAM IS A WISH YOUR HEART MAKES

Words and Music by MACK DAVID,
AL HOFFMAN and JERRY LIVINGSTON

# STRONG

Words and Music by PATRICK DOYLE,
KENNETH BRANAGH and TOMMY DANVERS

In a per-fect sto-ry-book ___
life's a dif-f'rent game, ___

the world is brave ___ and good: ___ a
the sor-row and ___ the pain. ___

he-ro takes ___ your hand; ___ sweet love will fol-
On-ly you ___ can change ___ your

*Recorded a half step higher.
†Melody is written an octave higher than sung.

# BIBBIDI BOBBIDI BOO
## (The Magic Song)

Words by JERRY LIVINGSTON
Music by MACK DAVID
and AL HOFFMAN

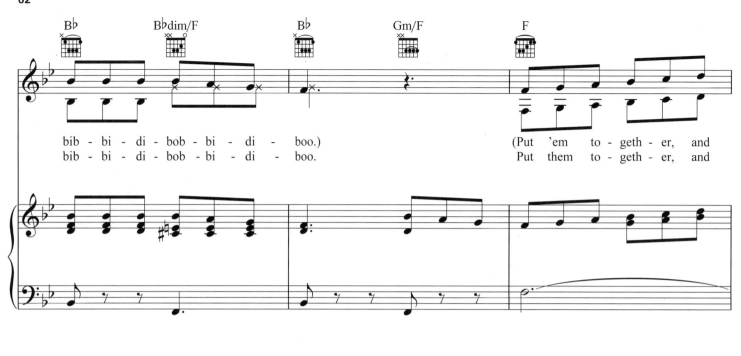

bib - bi - di - bob - bi - di - boo.)
bib - bi - di - bob - bi - di - boo.

(Put 'em to - geth - er, and
Put them to - geth - er, and

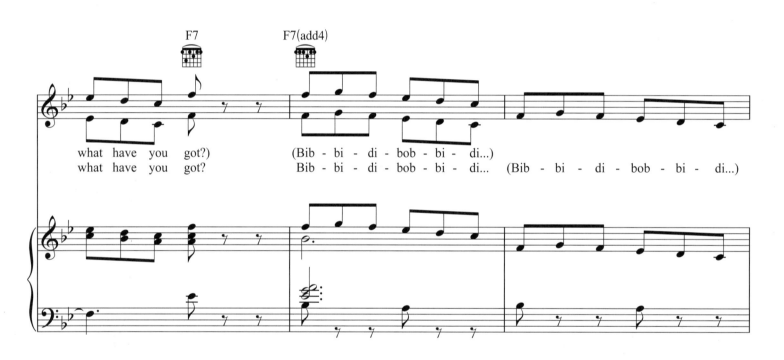

what have you got?)
what have you got?

(Bib - bi - di - bob - bi - di...)
Bib - bi - di - bob - bi - di... (Bib - bi - di - bob - bi - di...)

Bib - bi - di - bob - bi - di - boo! _____